Guess What

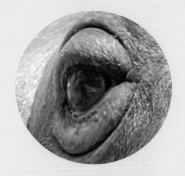

Peachtree

Published in the United States of America by
Cherry Lake Publishing
Ann Arbor, Michigan
www.cherrylakepublishing.com

Content Adviser: Susan Heinrichs Gray
Reading Adviser: Marla Conn, ReadAbility, Inc.
Book Designer: Felicia Macheske

Photo Credits: © BMJ/Shutterstock Images, cover, 15; © Elena Yakusheva/Shutterstock Images, 1, 8, 12; © Potapov Alexander/
Shutterstock Images, 3, 4; © NATALIA61/Shutterstock Images, 7; © Vladimir Melnik/Shutterstock Images, 11, 21; © Denis Burdin/
Shutterstock Images, 17; © Dr. J. Beller/Shutterstock Images, 18; © Andrey_Kuzmin/Shutterstock Images, back cover; © Eric
Isselee/Shutterstock Images, back cover

Library of Congress Cataloging-in-Publication Data

Macheske, Felicia, author.
Big and blubbery : walrus / Felicia Macheske.
pages cm. — (Guess what)
Summary: "Young children are natural problem solvers and always looking for answers, especially when it involves animals. Guess
What: Big and Blubbery: Walrus provides young curious readers with striking visual clues and simply written hints. Using the photos
and text, readers rely on visual literacy skills, reading, and reasoning as they solve the animal mystery. Clearly written facts give
readers a deeper understanding of how the walrus lives. Additional text features, including a glossary and an index, help students
locate information and learn new words"— Provided by publisher.
Audience: K to grade 3.
Includes index.
ISBN 978-1-63470-719-0 (hardcover) — ISBN 978-1-63470-749-7 (pbk.) — ISBN 978-1-63470-734-3 (pdf) — ISBN 978-1-63470-764-0
(ebook)
1. Walrus—Juvenile literature. 2. Children's questions and answers. I. Title.
QL737.P62M25 2016
599.79'9—dc23
2015026123

Cherry Lake Publishing would like to acknowledge the work of The Partnership for 21st Century Skills.
Please visit *www.p21.org* for more information.

Printed in the United States of America
Corporate Graphics

Table of Contents

I have small eyes for my big body.

I have
flippers
that help me
get around.

I have a lot of whiskers.

My thick blubber keeps me warm.

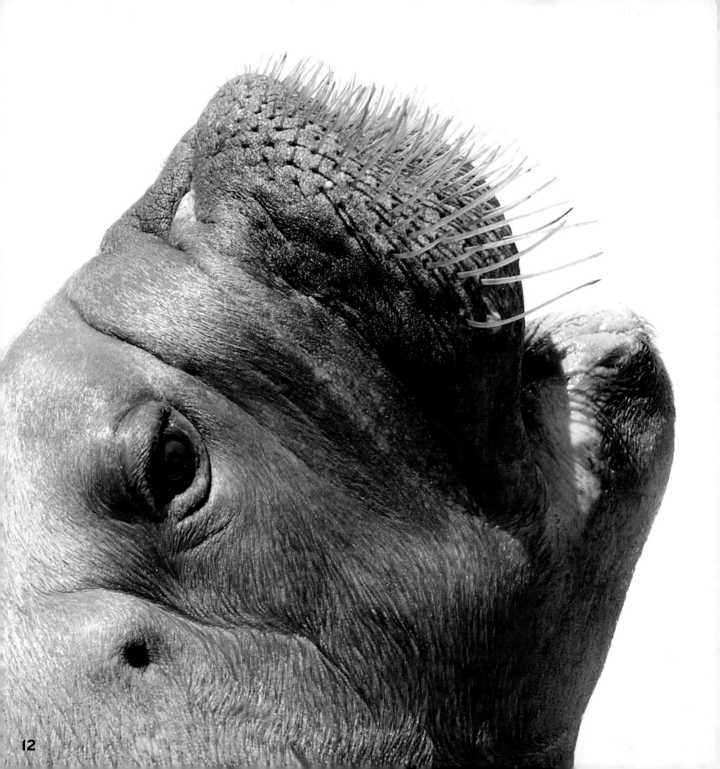

I can get very noisy.

I can grow very long tusks.

I live where it can get very cold.

Brr!

I am a good swimmer and like the water.

Do you know what I am?

I'm a Walrus!

About Walruses

1. The whiskers on a walrus are called a mustache.

2. Both male and female walruses can have tusks.

3. Walruses use their tusks for many things. One is to pull themselves out of the water.

4. Most walruses live near the Arctic Circle. It is very cold there.

5. A group of walruses is called a herd.

Glossary

blubber (BLUHB-ur) the layer of fat under the skin of a large sea animal

flippers (FLIP-urz) broad, flat body parts that sea animals use for swimming

noisy (NOY-zee) loud

tusks (TUHSKS) long, curved, pointed teeth that stick out of the mouth of some animals

whiskers (WIS-kurz) long, stiff hairs near the mouth of some animals

Index